Title: Independent Filmmakers Handbook

ISBN-13: 978-1-942825-39-5

Independent Filmmakers Handbook teaches you how to produce and distribute an independent film. This book is a must have for film students and independent filmmakers.

Author: Kambiz Mostofizadeh

Publisher: Mikazuki Publishing House

Introduction

I bought my first moviemaking camera when I was 22 years old. It was a Sony with night vision and all of the cool features I was looking for. I would convince anyone I could find to play in my films; classmates, friends, anyone. I made 25 short films before I was 25 years old and generated a buzz about my independent films. People still ask me about my films from when I was 21. I am embarrassed about them but people still do ask to see them. I bought a video mixing console from Radio Shack and I would add a score and sound effects to various scenes. I invested time and money in developing my art. The movies were hilarious and usually based around the horror genre. I was just trying to learn and get experience doing it. Please go to IMDB and search for Kambiz

Mostofizadeh, which is my full name. I have produced a reality television show in Las Vegas as well as various short and feature films. There is no secret formula to success but there are moviemaking fundamentals that have to be learned and applied in the creation of a film. There are so many specializations in the movie industry that you could not master them if you spent 3 lifetimes. You have to keep learning as much as you can so that you increase your understanding and knowledge of filmmaking. Buy as many books as you can on the subject and keep yourself updated. I learned a lot over the course of the creation of various short and feature films and this book is the culmination of what I have learned over the years.

Filmmaking Understanding

1. A movie is entertainment. You are not going to make Gone With The Wind with $500 and that is okay.

2. If somebody doesn't like your work, then tell them to change the channel. You are not responsible for the happiness and fulfillment of others. You are responsible for yourself and that is all.

3. Not being accepted should be acceptable to a true artist. You are not trying to be a crowd-pleaser.

4. Be realistic about your budget and what you can do with it. It is not about having more money, it is about sourcing things for less. Having more money

doesn't help you when you have to pay more for everything.

5. Plan each scene in detail with expenses noted for each item in the scene and a sum total for that scene.

6. Understand that you have to just make great scene. Since a movie is a collection of scenes, just focus on making one really great scene.

7. The only people that will not accept you are people that are either jealous of you or people that hate themselves.

8. You have to be willing to invest in your own film. Unless you invest in it first, no one else will.

9. Create alliances with people also in the movie industry to help you in your movie. You could offer a Director of Photography credit and/or deferred payments if they agree to bring their filmmaking equipment and participate.

10. Give people a reason to join your movie. Everyone wants to be a part of the winning team. Project success and believe in your near future success.

The 6 Stages of Filmmaking

Development – In the development stage you are preparing your script, creating storyboards, finding locations for filming, and putting together your cast and crew. The beginning is of utmost importance and should be given the most attention so that the project starts correctly.

Pre Production – In the pre production stage, the necessary permits that are required for filming are taken care of, the film insurance is purchased, the locations are confirmed, the sets are prepared, the costumes are sourced, and the financing is secured.

Production – In the production stage, the magic occurs. Scenes are created with lighting and sound using a prepared cast and crew.

Post Production – In the post production stage, the film footage is professionally edited, sound effects are added, scoring is added, visual effects are added, the titling is added, and the credits are added.

Distribution – In the distribution stage, film distributors are used to place your film in various channels. Film Festivals are an early form of distribution that increases your chances for success.

Marketing – In the marketing stage, you will spend all of your time using public relations, social media marketing, and advertising to generate sales. Filmmakers are not exempt from doing marketing labor.

Creating a Team

You may need 8 people to play in your movie. You may need 20 people or 100 people to play in your movie. Where are you going to get these people? The best place to start is where I started off looking for people to play in movies, the theater departments of universities and community colleges. I found my first actors and actresses in the acting classes I took at Los Angeles Pierce College in Los Angeles, California. I would strike up a conversation with the actors and actresses after acting class was over. I would tell them about a movie I am making and I would ask them if they would like to be in it. I would get their full names and phone numbers and I would build rapport with them. When I wanted to start the actual movie making on a Saturday, I would call them and invite them to meet me at a location. The first short action movies I made were in the wooded hills on the giant Pierce College campus. I would approach people randomly in the street if I thought they looked the part to be a character actor or actress. It is important to have a positive and upbeat attitude that is flexible to meeting new people and interacting with them. In other words, start socializing and build contacts from it. The difficulty is not finding people to help you in your movie. The difficulty is in being able to choose which ones are useful and productive and which ones will slow down or hurt your movie making process. The more people that you become acquainted with the more options you will have to choose from when you start the development phase of your movie.

Acting In Your Own Movie

You should create original characters to play in your own movie. When an Actor plays himself in a movie, then he has already broken the 4th Wall making the audience feel uncomfortable. The 4th Wall is the imaginary line or wall between the individuals performing in a movie and the viewing audience in a cinema or at home. There is a reason why actors play other characters and there is a reason why Actors don't look directly in to the camera, it is so they don't break the 4th Wall. Humans want to escape from reality which is why they watch movies in the 1st place. Humans watch movies to escape from reality, not to be pulled further in to the crappy reality that they're seeking to escape from. Secondly, when the tempo and pace is off in a scene, it is because the Director was un-willing to tell the Actors what to do (a recipe for disaster). Finally, if you as a Screenwriter can't come up with witty original content, then you should stop forcing Actors to memorize your material. Improvisation is more authentic and the meaning of that scene can still be conveyed without sacrificing quality in the dialogue. Yesterday's A list actor is now a C list actor. You can get half of these 90's stars for like $10,000 right now. But this is what Filmmakers will never understand. There is no Actor that is at the top forever just like there is no Actor (or Actress) that is at the bottom forever. In a movie, you have a Protagonist. That is the Good Guy. That is who you are rooting for to win, to succeed. The Bad Guy is called the Antagonist. The Protagonist is either a Hero or is an Anti-Hero, but they are still the Good Guy of the movie (Protagonist). An example of an Anti-Hero and my personal favorite is Snake Plissken from Escape From New York and Escape from L.A. The reason why Snake Plissken is an Anti-Hero is because he is the Protagonist but is forced in to this position (not of his own free will) and he hates the people that he is fighting for. In the movie Escape From New York, Snake

Plissken is the Protagonist (the Good Guy) sent in to rescue the President of the United States whose airplane landed in New York. Authenticity is better than having good looks. One being lowest 10 being best. Sometimes having two 5's in a scene is better than having one 10. And that 10 might be a look of a 10 with an attitude and personality of a 2. Communications between humans in any given scene is more important than looks. With the advancement of surgery, any actor or actress can look like anyone. You can take a 3 and make her a 10 if you spend $100,000 sculpting her face and body. There are actors that are a 7 or 8 and that is because they haven't spent $200,000 to look a 10. It is important to create unique characters that are authentic. Don't play ridiculous stereotypes like those used in Hollywood where Blacks are shown as thugs and losers, Mexicans are not even shown or if you are it is as a tank top wearing Gangster, Asians are shown as weak and vulnerable, Whites are shown as hillbilly backwoods villagers, and whoever Hollywood doesn't like is made to be the bad guy. Don't play stereotypes. Stereotypes are cliché and worn out. Be original and use your creativity to do so. Because movies can condition us, we have to be mindful of not playing in to the use of clichés and stereotypes. Films condition us based on the biases of the Screenwriter, Script Supervisor, Producer, and Director. Is this being done consciously or subconsciously? Depends on who is creating the film and depends on who is funding it. Movies sell an image by painting one person or group as the Protagonist (Good Guys) and one person or group as the

Antagonist (Bad Guys). This is how Storytelling works and according to time tested tradition in a 3 part Story Arc, the Good Guy has to win and the Bad Guy has to lose. It is a morality tale because Storytelling was traditionally the art that spread humanistic values. When the Producer and Director are told on the set that they must change lines in the script to make it more malleable to viewers, this affects Creativity and bypasses Creative Control. Acting is about authenticity. Acting is about having the correct behavior. The actor's behavior must be authentic and the actor must know the lines by memorization. Character actors just play themselves and they allow the qualities of that character to be automatically projected on to them. If you try to purposefully act as a character, it could come off as being inauthentic and phony. The best character actors just play themselves and they allow the qualities of that character to be projected on to them through the dialogue. For example, if you were going to play an Italian-American actor in the Bronx in the 1960's, you wouldn't act a certain way or walk a certain way (though you might have to talk a certain way as in with an accent), you would just play yourself and based on the surroundings and the environment, the audience would assume your role in it. If I am going to play a Puerto Rican in Miami, I may dress a certain way and talk with an accent, but I would not do anything else different than play myself. I would allow the audience to assume based on the surroundings. The audience would first notice that I am playing a Latin character and the surroundings of Miami would be natural to character. I would have to learn the accent by watching and mimicking the accent of native Miami speakers with a Latin background. In the 1970's mainstream comedy Airplane, Barbara Billingsley flew to the South to learn the Jive (Black Vernacular) accent used by African-Americans so that it would be authentic on film. Authenticity is the rule that should always be adhered to. I wouldn't walk a certain way or act any different than myself. I would let the audience assume and that itself is a powerful tool for connecting the imagination of the audience with that of the screenwriter. Acting is about doing what a person would naturally do in that place and time. A drill that is very effective for increasing your acting ability is the 2 Way Interaction. If you are asked a question, you repeat their question with a question. For example, if a person asks or even tells you a statement, you then reply to that question or statement with a question of your own. For example, if a person tells you that you look excited, you would reply with "I look excited?". This causes the conversation to build back and forth with questions in order to generate greater interaction between both actors. A dialogue is an interaction with two people, and most films you will watch feature a dialogue. The interaction is built by questions and statements, in order to create deeper and more meaningful communication between both of the actors. This technique is a powerful acting technique that will allow you to create simple and natural dialogues for your films. To become a better actor, you have to practice certain drills to help you improve. The 2 Way Interaction is a very powerful tool for developing your impromptu acting ability. Another powerful tool for developing your acting ability is the Observation Lens. In the Observation Lens drill, you should pick out a few places to choose from to visit. These places should be public and should allow you to watch others. The purpose of the Observation Lens drill is to watch how people move, how people talk, how people walk, and how people communicate. Are these people actors? No. They have no reason to act. They are people going about their business as usual. You have to become as natural on camera as they are natural going about their ordinary lives. The movements you make have to be as natural as the people you will observe living their lives. Acting is not about playing someone else, acting is about playing yourself with a few additions to increase authenticity. Those additions include wardrobe, accent, mannerisms (if natural and not exaggerated), and behavior (must be natural and not exaggerated). Natural acting creates authenticity and a direct connection with the audience. It is important to note that theater acting is different than film. In theater acting the audience is sitting frozen on one side. In film, the camera could move 360 degrees and capture the entire scene. The fundamentals of acting do not change but rather the angles. A drill that is of benefit to actors is repetition of phrases. The repetition of phrases allows for different tonal accents and different meanings. For example, let us choose a simple phrase such as "I feel hungry". Three words. Very simple. I feel hungry. Say this many times. Change the tone and the meaning. I feel hungry could be a statement. I feel hungry could be a question.

You can change the meanings of words by repeating them. The most important element to remember is to stay natural. What would the character you are playing naturally be doing? What movements are not natural for that character? What movements are natural for that character. You are not playing a character, you are becoming that character by taking on the internal and external traits of that character. If anyone sees that character they have to see you and if they see you they have to see that character. You morph in to that character and take on any qualities that character has without presenting it in a personified manner. You naturally become that character by understanding everything there is to know and learn about that character. What does your character love and what does your character hate? Does your character have any eccentricities? What motivates your character on a daily basis? What makes your character want to win? What makes your character different than other people around him or her? Where was your character raised as a child and in what condition were they raised? You have to think the character through and know everything about them. The scriptwriter created a character but the actor or actress brings that character to life. For example, let us say that I wanted to play the role of a Boxer. I would have to learn Boxing, train Boxing every day, get in to a Boxing sparring match, and learn about the history of Boxing. I would have to be that Boxer. But I would also have to know about the socio-economic background of that Boxer. I would have to know which culture that Boxer originally came and to attempt to learn their accent. I would want to travel to where that Boxer grew up and hang out with the locals there and speak to them. I would have to live and think like that Boxer so I could accurately depict that person in reality and on screen. I have to know my material inside and out. I would have to become them and really be them. I would practice their lines until I could recite them in my sleep. I would practice their tones and accent until I have mastered it. You have to take acting seriously because it is what the camera is capturing. Let's say you wanted to say "I feel young today". A simple phrase. I feel young today. Say that phrase over and over and over again. The phrase "I feel young today" takes on a new meaning. I feel young today can be expressed in amazement, "I feel young today!". I feel young today can be expressed as a question, "I feel young today?". I feel young today can be expressed sarcastically "I feel young today". I feel young today can be expressed soberly and straightforward without any tones, "I feel young today". The more you say "I feel young today" the more the sentence will change because your tones will change over time. This is an important acting drill that you should practice often. Your greatest ability will always be the ability to use your imagination. It is your duty as an actor to truthfully depict a character but you have to be able to use your imagination on areas where you are in doubt. Acting is about naturalism and doing what is natural at that place and time. Un-natural movements or personification introduce falsity in to the performance. Even if the character is not 100 percent accurate as to the original, the character still must be authentic in their actions. The character has to improvise and use their imagination to fill in the blanks on the areas where they are in doubt. Imagination is the greatest tool in the actor's arsenal and they have to use it in an impromptu way. An actress in a horror movie should not act scared. An actress in a horror movie should really be scared. The actress is not playing a woman scared because that would be phony and inauthentic. She has to really be scared in order for her feeling to pass on to us. Directors can easily discern between bad and good acting because they have experienced the difference. Actors and actresses have to be given as real a set as possible so that their feelings are felt at home by the viewing audience. Remember that the viewing audience is represented by the protagonist of the film. In the original Texas Chainsaw Massacre horror movie, the crew was kept up for 24 hours and an actress was chained to a chair in a dungeon like room. They really were disoriented and frightened and that showed on the screen in the final product. The actress in a horror movie should be made sensitive, disoriented, and vulnerable so that this feeling transpires in to cinematic art. If you want the audience to feel the horror The angry martial artist punching a heavy bag in a gym should not act angry. Let us say the lines are "I am angry" and then the martial artist punches the heavy bag. Saying this line without really feeling angry will come off as fake. It will come off as not being authentic and realistic. The actor should sit aside before filming and think about something that has made him angry in the past. The ability to draw out emotions instantly is a draining and difficult skill that experienced actors and actresses possess. Acting creates moods as each scene creates a specific mood. A mood has to be realistic. Fake enthusiasm is lacking in depth and substance. It has to be realistic above all. Fake tears are fake. If an actor wants to cry they have to summon up a memory that made them cry in the past. They have to really cry on camera, not fake cry on camera. Visine tear drops are not a substitute for real emotion. Real emotion will show up on camera and it will be felt by the audience watching. This is why fake tear drops do not create real emotion. Real tears and real crying make you shiver.

Cinematic Vision

You have to have cinematic vision and create

something original. Let us say you had the budget to re-create an action scene from The Terminator and the action scene looked fantastic. All you did was re-create a scene that has already been created. You did not do anything new. You did not do anything innovative or fresh. You just copied someone else. Originality is what makes your favorite filmmaker loved. Look at Stanley Kubrick. His films were all about originality and even his space movies introduced a new twist. Cliché is tiring and hard to watch. Originality makes an artist stand out from a crowd and allows them to develop a following. You cannot develop a following by being a carbon copy of what already exists. You are just being a me-too and there is no prestige or differentiation in that. You have to bring originality to the cinema and introduce new and fresh innovations that will stay in the mind of the moviegoer. Hitchcock was a master of macabre but it can be argued that he invented the horror movie genre. The introduction of paranoia in a character or helplessness are all features of today's modern horror films. Hitchcock brought more originality through Psycho which featured a cross dressing psychopath murdering his own hotel patrons. Original stories, original cinematography, and original acting made Hitchcock films stand out. Today's filmmakers are lacking in cinematic vision. The special effects are there and the acting is there but the plot is thin and not realistic. Realism is a factor that has been replaced by CGI and visual special effects. Cinematic vision is about being able to do what is fresh and innovative while being able to present the orthodox. Hitchcock would present the mundane and twist it. Everything would see normal at first and then one scene would change the film and take it in to a new direction (while still following the 3 Act Story Arc).

Storyboarding helps bring the cinematic vision to life and to provide a visual guide for the Director. Storyboarding is but a tool for visualization but the cinematic vision has to have relevance to the audience to prevent being an abstract art-house cinema film. For example, a movie about a poet wandering in a desert will probably have little relevance to a wide audience. It would be viewed as an abstract art-house theater cinema film with a narrow fan base. If you are comfortable with that style of film then you should proceed with that style. For those of us that seek to make a film that will be viewed by the widest audience possible, we want to make a movie in which the audience finds a connection with the protagonist (and if possible the antagonist). This connection provides a deeper meaning in to the film and draws us in to the film so that we feel that we are living through one of the characters. We want to experience our lives through their lives. Many women watch movies about castles because they dream of living in a castle. It is a play on our subconscious but we allow it because we understand that it is for entertainment purposes. You have to cast the widest net possible to catch the most fish. You are not going to become famous and rich off some abstract art-house theater cinema film production. It is not about budgets, it is about relevance. Can a large section of the global population, U.S. population, Canadian population, Australian population, English population, Irish population,

Scottish population, Indian population connect with one or two of the main characters on a personal level? What do those characters have that makes them connect with humans? The connection with the protagonist and/or with the antagonist pulls people in to cinemas. At one time, I was struck with Gold fever. I would check global Gold prices daily. I would read news about Gold. I would research Gold stocks. I saw an advertisement for a movie about Gold featuring Matthew McCaughey as a Gold speculator. I was beside myself with excitement to watch it! I connected with the protagonist, a Gold speculator and miner, who wanted to find Gold. The connection with the protagonist made me want to see the movie. For some people the connection with the antagonist makes them want to see the movie, such as fans of The Joker. Cobra Kai, a highly successful television show, based on The Karate Kid saga, has people attracted to the antagonists represented by the Cobra Kai dojo started by Sensei John Kreese. The protagonist, represented by Daniel LaRusso, has questionable character flaws but is invested in representing the good. The protagonist should be realistic in that they possess character flaws like other normal humans. Sometimes that is the only connection that is needed to draw in an audience. Even if the protagonist is weak and incompetent, the audience still cheer for the protagonist to win because they represent what is good in the story. The protagonist should be flawed which is a normal and natural way of humans. It makes the protagonist relatable to audiences. Clark Kent (of Superman) was very relatable to audiences. A normal city guy that goes to work 9 to 5 and does good in the community. The twist is when the glasses come off and he transforms in to a superhuman with superhuman abilities. At least one of the personalities of the character should be easily relatable and understandable without any mysteriousness to that character. That same character can change uniforms and personalities and become an entirely different person by way of the transformation. Dr Jekyll and Mr Hyde is a perfect example of a character that is normal and relatable to audiences. A medical doctor at work going through the usual tasks they carry out. The medical doctor changes in to a beast at night and that is the insertion of the Supernatural Effect. A normal scene is changed and altered through the addition of a supernatural element. A human can fly, run faster than a speeding bullet, and has come from a planet from Outer Space. That is most certainly supernatural and extraordinary. Normal is Clark Kent, the hard working urban clock watcher.

Suspension of Disbelief

People have to have a reason to part with their hard earned dollars. The large majority of people that watch a movie are doing so to forget about the problems in their own life. People watch movies to escape from reality. People don't watch movies to get depressed. People watch movies to get entertained and to change their mood. People don't watch movies to feel worse afterwards. People are paying to watch a movie to feel better afterwards. The happy ending serves to leave the audience in a cheerful and happy mood. Different genres require audiences to suspend their disbelief. A giant monster is running at the small protagonist in the woods and the small protagonist defeats it with a tree branch. People want to believe that the good guy wins because life itself is a morality tale. Furthermore, from a young age we have been conditioned with morality tales and the belief that the good guy has to win and the bad guy has to lose. Our art, our cinema, everything reflects this belief. The good guy gets the woman, gets the trophy, gets the treasure, and makes it back in time to teach classes. Even if that was not going to be the ending, we want a happy ending so we demand that the filmmaker allows us this privilege. The unspoken and unwritten contract that the audience makes with the filmmaker is to suspend their disbelief for the amount of time that they are watching the movie.

The audience wants to leave the confines of their reality and to enter the life of a person living in a castle or partying in college or running a marathon. The audience wants to do what they are unable to do in real life. Because the audience wants to escape from reality, the filmmaker has to provide the audience with a happy ending. The 3 Act Story Arc is just as relevant today as it was 500 years ago. People will suspend their disbelief willingly in order to be entertained. When you watch a magic show and the magician is sawing a woman in half, you know that it is make-believe. You know that the magician is not committing murder on stage by killing a woman by sawing her in half. It is entertainment and you and the rest of the audience do willingly suspend your disbelief in order to be entertained. This is why you should not be fearful of being experimental and doing new things. You may do something completely innovative but you have to be comfortable with doing things, whether they make sense or not. The audience will suspend their disbelief in order for it to make sense. We obviously know that humans cannot fly, but we do not question it in Peter Pan because his environment has its own rules that make flying acceptable. When we watch movies based on comic books, we do not question or second guess the reason why a human can change their skin to look someone else. We accept it because in that world of comic book heroes it is acceptable to have superhuman powers. We willingly suspend our disbelief because we understand that we are doing it for entertainment purposes. We do not believe in real life that humans can fly but we will accept it in a movie setting because we want to be amazed. We want to be amazed and tricked even for a moment, because it takes away from the harsh realities of life. We want to be amazed and dazzled. We want to be fooled for the amount of time we are watching the movie because we understand that we are being fooled for entertainment purposes. It is enjoyable to suspend your disbelief and we understand that by doing so we are going to be rewarded by being entertained. We suspend our disbelief in order to be amazed. It is like watching a magic trick. We want to be fooled for a short time. Because we want to be fooled for a short time, we are willing to believe just about anything while we are watching the movie. Some horror movies feature the bad guy being killed over and over yet still being able to come back from the dead. We believe that he could have come back from the dead or we do not question it at all. We are willing to go along with it because we understand that it is part of the entertainment. It is a part of the story and it has to believed or none of the story can be believed. We cannot accept some of the story. We have to accept the entire story or not accept it at all. We accept it at face value or we have to walk out the movie theater. There have been several times a movie was so bad that I did indeed walk out the movie theater. Most people wouldn't do that at all. They would go along with the premise because they are paying to be entertained. If you told them the sky is blue they would agree the sky is blue because the film is showing the sky to be blue. The film represents and even dictates their reality for the amount of time that they are watching the movie. The audience at a magic show do not want the magician to fail even if they think he or she is a bad magician. The audience in a movie theater wants the good guy to win, the bad guy to lose, the Woman has to be saved, the treasure must be gotten, and there has to be justice. This is because the 3 act story arc is ingrained in our psyche. It is after all a morality tale and the good guy has to win. Even though the 3 act story structure should be followed the screenwriter should be creative in creating twists, turns, and cliffhangers, so that the film becomes exciting. The wilder the better and it will not affect the believability of the audience because they have already agreed to believe anything that you will present to them. Do not be afraid to experiment and try out new things on camera. You never know when you might deliver lines in a way that might amaze you and your audience. You have to be willing to try new things on film and to be innovative. The beauty of acting and filmmaking is in the discovery and discovery only comes about during experimentation on film.

Building a Protagonist

The protagonist is the good person of the story. The protagonist is the hero or heroine of the story. They are the ones that will go through a herculean struggle to defeat their opponents and win. The protagonist does not have to archetypal. The protagonist in Spiderman, Peter Parker, is a nerd-ish bookworm that couldn't find a girlfriend if he tried. During calm he is the bookish coy Peter Parker, during trouble he is able to save human beings and stop evil. The normal was blended with the abnormal to achieve innovation. The orthodox was blended with the unorthodox to create something new, a 2 sided character. What if Superman never changed clothes and just had 1 side, the bookish Peter Parker with superhuman abilities that are hidden. The story would not have the same impact that it does today and the protagonist would not have the same impact that Peter Parker has. We love Peter Parker, not because he is Spiderman with superhuman abilities, but because he has the ability to be 2 people at the same time, bookish and aggressive (as two polar opposites). The protagonist is engaged in conflict and this conflict defines and creates the protagonist's powers (or develops their powers) allowing them to defeat the antagonist. The protagonist is engaged in this conflict in a few forms:

1. Man vs Man – The classic formula used so many times in Hollywood action movies.

2. Man vs Machine – The Terminator is a perfect example of a film where the protagonist is engaged in a conflict with a machine known as a terminator.

3. Man vs Nature – The Edge with Alec Baldwin and Anthony Hopkins is a perfect example of a man vs nature movie.

4. Hybrid – Cliffhanger is a movie that uses both man vs man and man vs nature. Predator is another example of a movie that features both man vs man and man vs nature.

Building an Antagonist

The bad guy has to be really bad. The worse in character that the bad guy appears the more the good guy will appear as the savior of everyone. It is not enough to say "the bad guy is bad". The bad guy has to be shown to the audience for the truly despicable character that he or she is. You have to reveal the horrible traits and character flaws of the bad guy to the audience so that the audience recognizes who is good and who is evil. The antagonist has to be shown and revealed in his or her natural evil state. The antagonist doesn't have to start off as a bad guy. They can start off as a good guy that goes through an intense period in their life that makes them a bad guy. The antagonist has experienced certain events (which you can show as scenes in your film) and these events have shaped their perception and mentality. The bad guys can even be well intentioned good guys whose intentions are not shared by all. The antagonist in Superman, Lex Luther, is not really a bad guy but his intentions can be perceived as being bad or being against the wishes of all. The antagonist doesn't have to be boilerplate and textbook. You can change the antagonist to be some good and some bad but containing more evil than good. I call this the Anti-Villain. More evil than good but contains some good. The antagonist has to be more than anything, exciting. A charismatic villain like The Joker brings more than evil to the screen. The Joker brings entertainment and excitement with every word or line uttered. Just as the protagonist goes through a personal journey the antagonist also goes through a personal journey that defines how they view themselves and how they view the world around them. The antagonist can be prone to psychotic bits but if their sole modus operandi is murder then the antagonist is best suited for a horror movie (more than anything else). The Joker is genius like, moving between psychotic episodes, delusions of grandeur, and likes to imagine himself as a savior of sorts. Even an all evil antagonist like Jason Voorhees from Friday the 13th was once an innocent young boy that was teased and tortured by his peers. He didn't start off as evil but rather practiced evil as a means to punish those who had bullied and tortured him. In this way, audiences even cheered when the antagonist went after a protagonist. The audience got on the side of Jason Voorhees because they could connect with his story of seeking revenge after being viciously bullied (thrown in the bottom of the lake with a weight to his ankle). The vicious chainsaw wielding Leatherface was just a normal boy that was teased for his facial deformities. The revenge of Leatherface was to seek revenge on the beautiful that had bullied him. The audience was no less horrified but they made a connection, however slight, with the antagonist because they could understand how a person could want to retaliate against bullying. There has to be a connection, an invisible rope, between the audience and the antagonist just as there has to be a connection with the protagonist. The audience has to relate with them in order for the story to have meaning for them. It could be argued that the antagonist is more important than the protagonist because the antagonist defines the life of the protagonist. Like Yin and Yang, they are connected by destiny and fate.

Understandable

There are some independent films that are so abstract that the viewer doesn't understand what is happening or what happens at the end. A movie has to be understandable. In order to be understandable it has to take an orthodox approach and introduce unorthodox. For example, let us say you want to make a horror movie about a small town whose inhabitants turn in to human eating lizards at night. You would introduce the small town and show small town America as it is. Kid riding bike, Mother baking Apple Pie, the neighborhood town hall style Diner, and the kids baseball league playing. It would be normal for anyone watching the film until the transformation of humans in to lizards. This is the blending of the normal and abnormal or the blending of the orthodox and unorthodox. If you made a movie about a person stuck in a desert from beginning to end, that would be unorthodox. Where did this man in the desert appear from? Did he just transport in to a desert? What is the plot? Man in desert has to survive? If the film starts showing a man in the desert without showing how they got there or the circumstances that led to him being there, that would be a horrible movie. The movie has to be understandable therefore a premise has to be established. Survival just for survival's sake is not a movie, it is a few scenes of a movie. You have to understand the circumstances that created the conditions in order for the survival to make sense. There has to be a light at the end of the tunnel or a pot of gold at the end

of the rainbow. If the movie starts
with a man trying to survive in the
desert, there has to be an
introduction of the circumstances
that led to this as well as the
person responsible so that
survival finds meaning. The
survival is to get justice by finding
the person that put him in this
position. Survival for survival's
sake is not a movie. Even Rambo
had a happy ending in that
Rambo walked away with his
freedom. Some of David Lynch's
movies like Mulholland Drive are
so abstract that you leave
wondering what it was all about.
A movie should blend together
orthodox and unorthodox
elements together to create
something unique. Give a new
twist to something old. You
should be innovative, but not so
much that your movie becomes
unintelligible. You should be
creative but not so much that it
appears amateur (erratic camera

movements, shaky camera, etc). Blending the normal and abnormal is about changing the tempo of the film. For example, the movie starts with a focus on a family eating dinner and praying on the 1st floor of the house and shows the 2nd floor holding a secret that is shocking. A giant dragon lives on the 2nd floor. The normal family dinner scene portrays and presents the normal while switching to the abnormal dragon living on the 2nd floor. By blending together the normal and the abnormal you are able to achieve something new, innovative, and fresh. Being innovative depends on breaking away from the mundane. Creating something new demands having cinematic vision.

Script or No Script?

A good script can sell for $250,000 or more in Hollywood.

Some scripts have been sold for over 1 million dollars. A great script can make or break a movie. A movie script is the blueprint for the entire movie. From props, to actors, to camera angles. The script gives you what you need to make a movie. Some filmmakers will swear by a movie script. They think that having a movie script is the only way to proceed with a film. No script, no movie! Is this true? No, absolutely not. A lot of movies are made without a script. The Director understands the direction of each Scene and all of the Scenes have been planned beforeheand. The scenes are acted in an impromptu manner without the need for a script. I have made over 35 short and feature films and never used a script. I understood the scenes that needed to be filmed and I knew what each scene took. I had no paperwork. I put together scene by scene until I had all the scenes I needed to edit. You are not forced to have a script. If you are trying to get a movie deal and all you have is a short film, then you will be asked for a script by the movie producers you are speaking with. If you are unable to produce a script, you will not receive their support. If you are not seeking major movie production company support then you do not need a script. You should have each scene planned out with all the parts listed so that you know exactly which persons, props, and locations needed to be used. You cannot logistically plan for filming a scene if you have not planned out that scene in-depth beforehand. You have to understand what persons, props, and locations are needed to be listed on a Production Sheet with itemized listings of everything that is in that scene. A tally of the costs involved should be listed as well in order to better understand what each scene will cost you. You can obviously design scenes with little cost and save your budget for scenes that are more cost intensive. Either way, you are not forced to have a script if you choose to use impromptu acting dialogue. Impromptu acting dialogue makes the movie more realistic. This could translate to a greater connection between the viewing audience and the film. Impromptu acting dialogue is fresh and feels comfortable to the viewer. If you plan on using a script, each page of your script roughly represents on average 1 minute of screen time. A two hour movie would require 120 pages of screenwriting. There are various software programs that you can use that provide the screenwriting format and assist you with proper typsetting. Many persons still prefer no software and choose to go about it the old fashioned way (I like it like that!). Before the computer there was the good old fashioned typewriter and they churned out scripts just fine. Some writers still prefer to use a typewriter because of its romanticism. Before you write a script, you must understand what a script is. A script is a screenplay. Scripts are usually adapted from books. A script, as the screenplay, holds the direction of the film, the lines that the actors and actresses will memorize and recite, the camera shots, the cues for when a scene is cut, the cues for when a scene starts, when narration is used, etc. You should use abbreviations in your script so everyone can understand it. The following abbreviations will help you for use in your script.

SCRIPT ABBREVIATIONS

POV - Point of view shot

ELS - Extreme long shot

MLS - Medium long shot

LS - Long shot

MS - Medium shot

MCU - Medium close-up

CU - Close-up

ECU - Extreme close-up

OS - Over-the-shoulder shot

2S - Two shot

3S – Three shot

INT - Interior

ZI - Zoom in

ZO - Zoom out

SOT - Sound on tape

SOF - Sound on film

EXT - Exterior

CGI – Computer Graphic Image

SFX – Sound Effects

SPFX – Special Effects

BG - Background

OSV - Off-screen voice

VO - Voice-over

MIC - Microphone

MOS – Moment of Silence

OC – Off Camera Narration

DIS - Dissolve

Q - Cue

BEAT - Pause

VTR - Videotape

SUPER - Superimposition

ANNCR - Announcer

Low Budget vs High Budget

Major film studios spend hundreds of millions of dollars making high budget films. They believe that high budget films are the only ones that will achieve success. They are correct some of the time but not all of the time. There have been many high budget movies that have failed at the Box Office. For a myriad of reasons they failed. It could have been the story they chose. It could have been a weak plot. It could have been a weak market. For the most part, high budget movies that chose certain genres like Comic Book adaptation action movies have been successful. They have made their money back many times over generating billions of dollars from franchise movies they produce. If you have hundreds of millions of dollars, this book is probably not going to help you much. But if you are working with a small limited budget, then this book will help you make a short or feature film using less resources. Paranormal Activity was made with $15,000 and it grossed over $160,000,000 at the box office. Moviemaking is about being resourceful. Everyone knows how to waste money but few understand how to source similar quality products and services at a lower price. Working with a lower budget forces you to be more creative and more resourceful. Look at India's film industry known as Bollywood. They produce wildly popular movies that generate tons of money while using small budgets. Surely their movies are not as good as Hollywood movies. No one disputes that. Is the point of business to be better or is the goal of business to be more profitable? The goal of a business is to be more profitable. Indian movies are highly profitable because they use a small budget. If the movie has value, the audience will find it no matter how small the budget. A perfect example is The Blair Witch project that was made with less than $20,000 and generated millions of dollars in sales. The social media hype they generated created buzz among horror movie fans. It is not important to have a large budget rather it is important to be resourceful. One of the movies that I was an Actor in titled "The Other Black Guy Running For President", was wildly successful in its marketing because it launched during the 2012 Presidential Election, using that hype to generate interest. The movie was downloaded over 1 million times at $5.99 and became a definite success as an independent film production. You don't have to have a high budget, what you need is interesting and viewable content. If you can source everything you need at half the price why wouldn't you do that? You will do it because resourcefulness is the first rule of independent filmmaking. You have to work with what you have and you should only source items that are missing for a particular scene. Since you just have to start by shooting one scene at a time, you can just focus on sourcing what you need for that particular scene. More money doesn't mean your movie will be better. There are many horrible movies with bad acting that have been produced with large budgets. Don't fret about having a large amount of money. Learn to source what you need for much less and be resourceful by borrowing, bartering, renting, and outsourcing. Bollywood is viewed as being considerably low budget and low quality in comparison to blockbuster Hollywood movies. If that is the case, then why does Bollywood sell more movie box office tickets than Hollywood? Isn't Hollywood better? Isn't Tom Cruise or Matt Damon better looking than Shahrukh Khan? Then why does Bollywood sell more tickets than Hollywood? Shouldn't Hollywood be leading the pack? Tyler Perry has been falsely accused of making low budget Black comedies. Tyler Perry is a Billionaire. People are not there to watch your special effects. People are watching a movie to see humans. Now, if the human can shoot lasers from their eyes, great. If they can't, that is just as fine. There is no standard formula. You might hate Bollywood movies. 2 Billion people love Bollywood movies. You think your 100 million dollar budget is better than a low budget movie? Good for you. 2

Billion people still like Bollywood movies. 2 Billion like to see a beautiful feminine woman that is feminine and doesn't want to be a heroine. 2 Billion people movie fans like to see musical format mixed in to a movie, whether low budget or high budget. Bollywood can't make Iron Man and it doesn't want to make Iron Man. It wants to make movies about love, romance, action, adventure, comedy, and all the genres mixed together in one film. If there was a secret formula to movie success then there would be no need for Movie Producers. A movie would get made according to a formula and your success or defeat would be based on that formula. Remember the movie The Expendables? Did it not have top level actors and actresses in it? Why did it fail then? They thought they found the secret formula of successful moviemaking. Put in famous great actors. Get the best of everything. Spend millions of dollars on production. The result? Failure at the Box Office. Was it because the actors were not famous? There is really no way to fix a bad movie. The best way is to start with a clean slate and create a fresh movie. Hollywood makes moves based on the idea that it has some secret formula for movie success, which couldn't be further from the truth. The reality is that filmmaking is hit or miss. You either hit the target or you don't. An example of a hit and miss Hollywood movie is Cowboys and Aliens. I literally watched hundreds of people in multiple theaters laughing when they heard the name. It wasn't received well at the Box Office but went on later to do well on streaming platforms and DVD. There is no way of determining the success or failure of any art project, and filmmaking is indeed a complex art form. You have to do what you love and hope that others will share your love. Horror movie filmmaker George Romero was really in love with the style, tempo, and nuances of Horror films. Romero was in love with the art of making horror and that translated on to the screen and in to the hearts of moviegoers. You have to love what you are doing and be invested in the art of it so much that others will catch your inspiration. If you are in love with your movie then that enthusiasm will pass on to others because enthusiasm is contagious. Show your enthusiasm to the world and watch how quickly others will also become enthusiastic.

Funding Your Movie

You are either going to have to fund the movie yourself or you are going to have to raise money for your money. If you have $5,000, you can make a ultra-low budget horror movie. If you don't have $5,000, or you need much more than that amount, then you will have to raise the funds from interested investors. The movie business is like any other business, it is a business. You may be doing it for the love of it or for the art, but the only reason that anyone would want to get involved in your movie is because they think that they will benefit from it. They want to make money from it. Investors have to be found but if you are not a specialist in movie investment funding, then you will have to bring in a specialist that does expertise. You can pay them a small fee, say $500, and give them a commission on every dollar they raise for your movie. A good strategy would be to organize a movie fundraising event at a restaurant and invite the potential investors for a presentation. If you have all the different investors together in one place and give them a presentation, it makes your job easier and more efficient. Investors don't want to be left behind or miss out on the next big thing, and you have to hype the movie enough that they will believe that they will be left behind if they don't invest. Having un-related investors together in one place also creates a silent form of competition that will benefit you. You can also approach film venture capital companies and angel investors. Potential investors will always ask how much of your own money you have invested and how much this movie projects that it will gross. Investors, are after all, investors and the return on their investment matters more to them than what your story is. Investors want to see projections of sales and want to understand what their rate of return will be. They are seeking new ways to make money and if they allow you a meeting to pitch them it is because they also see themselves as being able to financially gain and jump on the bandwagon (so as to not get left behind).

The top ways that movies are funded are:

High Net Worth Investors – People will high net worth and with lots of money to invest. High Net Worth Investors make up the largest part of film financiers.

Product Placement – Brands are always seeking out new ways to get their brand names seen by greater audiences. Brands such as Hershey's paid 1 million dollars to have their Reese's Pieces brand featured in the mega-blockbuster movie E.T.

Brands such as Fed Ex worked with Tom Hanks to make an entire movie about a Fed Ex employee stranded on an island.

Crowdfunding – Sites like Kickstarter and IndieGogo provide crowdfunding services to filmmakers.

Pre-Sales – The distribution rights for various nations are sold to film distribution companies.

Grants – There are many non-profit organizations that are patrons of art and cinema. Grants, unlike loans, have the advantage of not having to be paid back. Grants take longer to secure and offer less money than other forms of funding.

Many film production companies use a combination of methods to raise money for their film including tax incentives, grants, and pre-sales of distribution rights. There is not one correct way to do it, rather film production companies use various ways to raise money for their films.

Genres

Which genre is best for you? Which genre should you choose for your next movie? According to Statista, from 1995 to 2020 these were the best selling movie genres in North America, in order of highest selling to least selling.

Adventure – 63 Billion Dollars

Action – 47 Billion Dollars

Drama – 36 Billion Dollars

Comedy – 34 Billion Dollars

Suspense – 20 Billion Dollars

Horror – 11 Billion Dollars

Romantic Comedy – 10 Billion Dollars

Musical – 4 Billion Dollars

Documentary – 2 Billion Dollars

Black Comedy – 1.5 Billion Dollars

There are fusion genres as well such as:

Action Comedy – Rush Hour featuring Jackie Chan is an example of a highly successful action comedy.

Musical Horror – Little Shop of Horrors is an example of a highly successful musical horror.

Adventure Comedy – Jumanji is an example of a highly successful adventure comedy.

Horror Comedy – Scary Movie is an example of a highly successful horror comedy.

Comedy Documentary – Bowling For Columbine is an example of a comedy documentary.

You can put together various genres and create your own genre. Some genres like Horror and Documentaries, have a higher return on investment than other genres. This is because horror movies cost considerably less to make than adventure movies. Adventure movies have a large return on investment but tend to be capital intensive. Documentaries have a high rate of return but are not capital intensive. Horror movies have a high rate of return but are not capital intensive. Ultimately, you want to choose a genre that fits your budget. If all the budget you have is $100, you might want to focus on making a Documentary. If all the budget you have is $500, an ultra-low budget horror movie is probably going to be your best option. Remember to be resourceful and work with what you have. Horror movies tend to be popular and have a high rate of return, which is why it is a great option for a beginning filmmaker.

Most Organized Wins

You have to get organized. You are not going to win by being un-organized. You have to know where everything is and how long it takes to access it. Major movie studios have professionally organized warehouses that hold movie equipment, movie props, and other items used in the process of filmmaking. They are organized and numbered. The information on that individual item is stored in an inventory database and is accessible by authorized personnel. Major movie studios are organized and ready to start a film production at any time. You have also be organized and have a simple inventory list that shows each item and its location. This way you will be organized. You have to take organization seriously as a production has to operate as a lean unit, capable of maintaining operations on an accountable budget. If you are not organized, you will waste money and time on frivolous activities or on extra items. Organization will act as a force multiplier, driving your production forward with minimal effort. The most organized wins and you have to spend a considerable amount of time making sure that you are organized and prepared.

Being organized means filtering out the noise and focusing on what is important. Being organized means removing all clutter so that you can access anything you need within the shortest amount of time.

How Many Cameras?

How many cameras do you really need to create a professional Hollywood like movie. Some would argue 2 cameras would be more than sufficient for the task. Some would argue 3 cameras would be ideal. If you can put together 3 cameras that would be ideal but if you can't, 2 cameras would be more than sufficient for achieving than your goals. You want to use 4K cameras at minimum. 4K cameras have at least 4000 lines of resolution, which is close to that of professional Hollywood cinematic cameras that have

5000 lines of resolution. Most film production companies have switched to 4k and 5k cameras to provide them with clear and crisp footage. You do not need to have a 35mm cinematic movie camera to make a short or feature film. Some feature films have been made with just a HD camera. Ultimately, what you are going to show is more important than the camera itself. Cinematic 4K cameras are not inexpensive but then again, movie making is not inexpensive. If you are passionate about filmmaking and you see yourself as a professional filmmaker, then you have to invest in professional camera equipment. If you have to pay it off monthly using credit then do it. You have to own your own equipment. If you own at least one 4k camera, then you can rent or borrow a second one. Not all 4k cameras are alike and you should spend a considerable time studying and researching the differences between them. You should watch stock video footage from the camera you wish to purchase and you should read many reviews about it in order to purchase a camera with confidence. You should invest in a good cardioid shotgun microphone with holder. You should invest in some form of portable lighting system. At the bare minimum you need 2 cameras, shotgun microphones, and a portable lighting system. I produced and filmed a reality TV magic show in the streets of Las Vegas using just a camera, shotgun microphone, and portable lighting system. Because it was filmed in one take, I did not need multiple cameras. I wanted each scene to be filmed in one take so that the audience would not think there was any "TV magic" involved in the magician's tricks. One camera, shotgun microphone, and portable lighting was sufficient for that production. The question of how many cameras comes down to your budget. Again, 2 cameras would be more than sufficient and 3 cameras would be ideal. Your scene, will most of all, determine exactly how many cameras you will need. A simple conversation can easily be filmed with 2 cameras but an intricate action sequence may require 3 cameras. If you are filming action sequences the majority of the time, then you might want to think about investing in 3 cameras. If you are not filming action sequences the majority of the time, 2 cameras will be sufficient for filming conversations between multiple people. The majority of your film footage will not be panning shots of backgrounds. The majority of your film footage will be used for filming dialogue between 2 or 3 or 4 or 5 people simultaneously.

Casting

Each actor or actress has a headshot with resume that you can find by contacting talent agents. You can also outsource the task of casting to a Casting Agency. There are a handful of famous casting agencies in Hollywood that get most of the business from the major film studios. A casting agency deals with the talent agencies representing the talent. Although the casting agencies carry out the task of sifting through and selecting talent, it ultimately up to the Film Production Company or producer to give the final go ahead. You can also do your own casting by setting up an audition at a location with a time and date. Many persons will appear with and without headshots with resumes. Casting is about finding the right face that also has the ability to pull of the role in question. In a typical casting agency audition, talent will appear and act out lines from the script (or a sample script created just for the audition). The casting directors are seeking acting ability as well as the right look. Sometimes having the right look has been more important than knowing acting. Many of the actors and actresses in Hollywood came from non-acting backgrounds such as modeling or manual labor. Steven Seagal was spotted by a talent agent in a martial arts class. He wasn't an actor. He learned acting to match his martial arts ability. The film industry has the ability and infrastructure to create actors and actresses. There are acting schools on practically every corner in Hollywood and there are bookstores such as Samuel

French bookstore that is focused on the acting industry. Casting agencies are experienced enough to correctly pick the faces and talent you are seeking while saving you the time, effort, and cost required to put together a large scale audition. Casting directors that have worked with major film production companies can bring that level of professionalism and expertise to your movie project.

Special Effects

Special effects add realism to a movie. They make the movie more enjoyable and more entertaining. For example, let us two individuals get in to a fight. After a punch is delivered, the hero starts bleeding from his right cheek. How is that blood going to be generated? Computer? Make up? Computer could be too costly for that scene so make up is applied. You have now used special effects to enhance the film. Make up is special effects? Yes. Make up is special effects. A cut to the face would be made with make up. If you want you can make it with a computer. Either way, the special effect of the hero bleeding from his right cheek has to be created using either a computer or a special effects make up artist. A special effects specialist applies the make up creating the looking of a bleeding right cheek. The hero pulls out a knife and cuts the bad guy. The special effects make up artist applies fake skin that re-creates the look of cut bleeding skin. The bad guy pulls out a lighter and throws it at some gasoline starting a fire and small explosion. A licensed pyrotechnics special effects specialist would create that special effect on set or the special effect would have to be created using a computer. Most film production companies cant afford to make Star Wars but they can afford to hire the special effects company that was responsible for Star Wars. Special Effects can make or break an action movie. A car catching fire after flipping in an action scene would require professional stuntmen or stuntwomen and it would need special effects (car catching fire). You can use CGI to create the fire special effects or you can use traditional pyrotechnics. A scene where two people are fighting each other in a gun fight would require special effects such as the bullets shown in air or the bullet being loaded in to the chamber of a gun. A CGI shark chasing people in a CGI ocean is one example of successful special effects. Animatronics that act as robots are another form of special effects. Visual special effects enhance the entertainment value of your film and bring prestige to it (if the special effects are professional and not cheesy). I personally prefer Zombies created with make up more than I do Zombies created with computer graphics. There is something more authentic about people with make up on made to look like Zombies. It looks and feel more realistic than computer graphic Zombies. Special effects are expensive depending on the scene you are attempting to create. The famous Lightsaber laser sword fight in Star Wars made George Lucas wildly famous. Special effects put us in awe and make us wonder more about science. More than anything, special effects can make us fall in love with a movie.

Cinematography

You will not understand cinematography until you pick up a camera and begin filming. You will learn how to properly frame a shot, how to zoom, how to pan, how to tilt, and what angles to use. Until you pick up a camera and gain experience, everything you learn will be for gaining knowledge purposes. You are learning in order to gain experience and skill required to create short films and feature films. Each shot should be simple and relaxed. Hurried shots, oblong shots, and erratic camera movements result in poor shots that are not usable for editing. You should use a long distance (far shot) shot to present the location, use mid-range shots to establish the scene, and use close shots to express emotion and communication. Too many shots in a short period of time during a two person conversation would be over-dramatic. Not enough shots during a two way conversation and it will become monotonous to watch. Two cameras can capture a two person conversation with ease, allowing for easy editing of the scene at a later time. It is okay to use long, mid, and near panning shots but erratic camera movements make the film seem amateur and un-professional. Use the standard long shot to present the location, mid shots to establish scene, and close shots for two way interaction. Putting together a planned sequence of shots with fast cuts is good for transitions. Too many angle changes during a two way interaction should be avoided. Use simple over the shoulder angles and keep the camera in a static position. The less you use your hands to hold the camera the better. Use a tripod and try to use simple but effective angles. Use test shots and review them to understand what the scene looks like on camera. Avoid low light shots and make sure that you have setup your portable lighting system beforehand. Using natural sunlight and filming outdoors provides the highest quality when recording. Low light shots become grainy and low quality, which is why day filming and using natural sunlight should be sought after. Natural sunlight provides you with clear crisp quality that almost makes $300,000 cameras and $400 cameras indistinguishable. Using an expensive camera is no guarantee of achieving success in your film. You have to be able to create new and interesting content that a viewing audience would enjoy. A slick clean production presents your scenes in a more connectable format.

Sound

Sound is just as important as visuals are.. You can use a shotgun boom microphone, small microphone like the Senheisser MKE 400, and lapel microphones. In addition, you can use voiceovers for characters. It is important that voiceovers are recorded in a professional studio with professional microphones in order to achieve crisp clear sound. Keep the treble and bass flat during recording so that they can be manipulated in post-production. You can use a portable battery operated 24 track recorder, a portable handheld digital audio recorder, or the camera to capture audio from microphones. It is important to only use clear audio and to have a sound engineer that can assist with sound recording. You can use multiple microphones like the Behringer C4 instrument microphone or one microphone. Multiple microphones are important because one of your microphones may malfunction during a recording session. Having two microphones insures that the scene will not be wasted. You should test the levels and do a test recording, before beginning the final recording. Sound is just as important as visuals are, which is why you should spend considerable time perfecting the sound levels so that they are at the optimum level for recording. Paying a professional sound engineer to oversee the sound of the film will give you many benefits such as clear audio through the reduction of unwanted noise.

Scoring

Music sets the scene. If you are showing a romantic scene, then light music like classical music or jazz would be more appropriate. If you are showing people in a party or a car chase, EDM music might be a better match for you. You want to try out different music to see which one matches better. There are many filmmakers like John Carpenter that make their own music. It is up to you to decide whether you want to make your own music or whether you want to purchase music from others. You could license the rights to a song for as low as $25. It depends on what song you want to use. Obviously, if you want to use a song by Mick Jagger it will cost you more than an unknown recording artist. Music Supervisors can be paid to pick out songs for you to use. You can also visit websites that specialize in licensing music for movies. Music sets the mood therefore it sets the scene. A fight scene would demand up-tempo musical scoring while a love scene may demand tender thoughtful heartwarming music. Each scene is unique and demands its own musical scoring. Watch David Lynch's Dune and compare that musical score with that of American Graffiti. Watch Grease and compare the musical score with that of Fame. Each movie has its own unique theme and style and demands an original score be composed to enhance the visuals. John Carpenter has famously composed music for so many of his films and has brought his own unique style and theme to his films. Escape From New York, Assault on Precinct 19, and The Thing have a unique sound that professional musicians would not have chosen. The sound may some a bit amateurish but it worked in the long run and John Carpenter became famous for his signature musical scoring style. If you possess musical production ability then you can score it yourself by renting out a music studio for 1 day. The music sets the moods for the scenes and makes them more enjoyable to watch which is why you should be very discerning in the songs that you choose. I created my scoring for my Do Aliens Exist documentary using a Korg Kaossilator synthesizer, 24 track digital recorder, and a Korg Electribe music production center. Since I owned my own music equipment and had many years of experience in music production, I opted to do my own scoring. I could have hired anyone of the many composers I know but I wanted my sounds to be the score. If you have the equipment available and you have the experience to do it yourself, it is best to do your own scoring. Some people are not in the position to do that and have to outsource the scoring to others. In most cases, scoring should be outsourced to music professionals with vast experience in music production for film. Making music is different than scoring a movie. Since each scene is trying to convey a particular mood, each scene absolutely requires its own style of score. It may cost you a few hundred or a few thousand dollars, but your movie will benefit from being scored professionally. It will add value to your film and make mundane scenes become exciting to watch.

Action Scenes

Fight choreography can greatly increase the quality of your film. Fight choreography is choreographed fighting between two persons or more and is used to add action to a scene. There are simple rules that should be used when using fight choreography and they include:

1. Safety First – Do not risk injury to each other. Practice with each other extensively.

2. Show Reaction – The viewing audience at home wants to feel the action. The fighter receiving a punch or kick or strike must show reaction when getting hit. The reaction should be bodily. For example, if you are getting punched in the stomach, your body should exhibit a reaction to that punch so that the viewing audience understands what has transpired. If your face is being punched, then your head should exhibit a reaction to the punch.

3. Use natural moves – Is it normal for an untrained fighter to suddenly start

performing complex moves? A character should only do moves that would be natural to that character.

4. Realism – The techniques have to be done in a way that is realistic to the viewing audience. Using reactions build realism.

5. Use Workable Techniques – Don't attempt moves that are too complex or too difficult to pull off. Focus on using workable techniques that are easy to do and easy to learn.

6. Use multiple takes – Film the fight sequence multiple times. Get used to performing the fight sequence and then watching the footage to

look for areas that can be improved.

7. Use Verbal Indicators – Use verbal noises to let the audience know you have been hit. A simple grunt when hit helps add realism to the scene.

8. Use larger movements on camera - A Jumping Knee, a Spinning Kick, etc. Larger movements translate better on film and are more exciting to the viewing audience.

9. Seek Perfection – The more times that you do the scene the more fluid you will become. Be willing to put in the time to reach perfection. The cast of the Matrix had to practice martial arts for 8 hours a day for 1 year to perfect

fighting sequences before filming.

10. Use fast shots – Fast shots in sequence add to the excitement of an action scene. Stringing together shots in a fast manner allows the viewing audience to see more. This is why it is important to try to have 3 cameras for an action sequence.

Some martial arts translate better on screen than others. Tae Kwan Do, Kung Fu, Karate, Aikido, Kendo, MMA, Wrestling, Muay Thai, and Boxing show themselves well on camera. Whatever style of fight choreography, it is important to practice, practice, practice until the scene arrives at fluidity and perfection. You could hire a professional fight choreographer for a few thousand dollars and it will really make a huge difference in your production. If you do not have access to the funds to do this then you should contact the Theater Department of a local Community College and ask for their help. Another option is to offer a fight choreographer credits and deferred pay in return for their services. Another option is to contact a few local martial artists or martial arts schools and ask them to get involved in the fight choreography for a few hundred dollars. Another option is to start learning martial arts and doing the fight choreography yourself by learning through trial and error. Whichever option you use, just remember, Safety First! Remember to have waivers signed by participants beforehand to prevent being sued in case of a serious injury. Professional fight choreographers deserve what they are paid because they can bring professional fight choreography to your production. Fight choreographers also help promote your film through various Social Media posts made during the production and after release. Fight choreographer Yueh Woo Ping was behind the success of many Asian action films and brought that expertise to The Matrix. I point out The Matrix regularly in fight choreography because of its meticulous attention to detail. Award winning Fight Choreographer Simon Rhee made Inception an amazing film to watch. Fight choreography excites the viewers and creates inspiration. Fight choreography made Creed great to watch. Fight choreography made Enter the Dragon great to watch. Fight choreography defined Hong Kong Kung Fu movies. Fight choreography made movies like Braveheart endearing to moviegoers. Films that have poor fight choreography are seen as low budget and low quality. A good fight choreographer can receive $50,000 or more for one week of work. An independent film themed around a martial arts master will benefit greatly using a professional fight choreographer with experience and a successful track record. A professional fight choreographer doesn't just teach punching and kicking on film. A professional fight choreographer can plan and create an entire action sequence that involves stunts.

Stunts

Stunts are dangerous feats that are performed on film. For example, the good guy falls from the second floor of a building and survives. A simple stunt such as this is in fact a very dangerous stunt that is only performed by professional stuntmen or stuntwomen. Not only meticulous planning goes in to its execution but there are aids such as a harness and giant inflatable mattresses used to protect the stuntperson during the fall. Amateurs have killed themselves or maimed themselves permanently attempting to perform stunts. Stunt work is highly dangerous work that is left up to professionals. You should not attempt stunts. You should not perform stunts. If you are doing even a simple jumping over a parking rail scene, it may be better if you bring in a professional stuntman or stuntwoman to do the task for you. It may seem costly but it is more costly to lose your life over a 2 second film shot. It is just not worth it, no matter how you look at it. If you need to do a street running chase scene, a person with Parkour training might be able to do the jumps for you. If you are doing a fighting scene, it may not be a bad idea to bring in someone with your height and weight that can perform movements that you are unable to do. It is always Safety First and you cannot be safe if you are attempting to perform stunts. All you can do is arrange for a safe environment that is approved by a professional stuntman or stuntwoman and ask them to perform the stunt while you film. Stunts like car chase require days if not weeks of planning for perfect execution and require proper permits before filming. Complex stunts take much longer to plan. A car chase takes place in public area and would absolutely require film permits and permits from various departments (Fire, Police, etc). A car chase requires professional stuntmen or stuntwomen with previous experience in performing similar stunts. Even a simple stunt like climbing a 10 foot wall would require a professional stuntperson because it would be dangerous to perform if you didn't have experience doing it before. Even if you had jumped a 10 foot wall once or twice in your life, you would not be able to perform it at fast speed while on camera and land on your feet safely. You could end up hurting yourself or watching one of your crew members hurt themselves. A professional stuntman or stuntwoman is required for safe stunt work. You may have to spend a few thousand, but professional stunts will increase the view-ability of your film. An un-professional stunt can lead to death or serious injury and should not be attempted by you or anyone in your crew. You should only use professionals to prevent injuries from occurring. Famous actors like Jackie Chan and Tom Cruise perform their own stunts. Tom Cruise has been seriously injured for months at a time after a stunt went wrong during the filming of the Mission Impossible movie series. Accidents happen often which is why you should only use experienced stuntmen or stuntwomen. A few thousand dollars spent on professional stunts is better than $100,000 spent on hospital bills for you and your crew members. Do not take unnecessary risks if you do not have to. Professionalism is about leaving the specialized tasks in the hands of competent experienced individuals with complete understanding in performing them.

Shots

Use angles that are simple. Complex shots are difficult and cost intensive. You may not have a crane available in the location you are filming. You may not be able to have access to a dolly, drone, or jib and crane. All you have are you cameras, tripods, lighting equipment, and sound equipment (microphone and/or external sound recorder). You have to use simple shots.

Very Wide Shot – Shows the entire scene from a very far distance so as to establish location.

Wide Shot – Shows the entire scene from a far distance.

Mid Shot – Establishes the premise of the scene and gives the viewing audience and understanding of the scene. Shows background and part of the subject.

Medium Close Up Shot – Shows the background but focuses close up on the subject.

Close Up Shot – Used in a dialogue scene to express two way interaction and emotion.

Extreme Close Up – Used to express extreme emotion such as showing the eyes of a character during a horror movie.

Low Angle – The camera is in a low position pointing up.

Worm's Eye View – The camera is in a very low position pointing up.

Straight Angle – Camera is at eye level.

High Angle – The camera is in a high position pointing downwards.

Bird's Eye View – The camera is in a very high position pointing downwards.

Over The Shoulder Angle – Camera is placed behind the shoulder of the subject.

Dutch Angle – The camera is tilted.

Point of View – The camera is in the 1st person position. Used to convey the mindset and vision of the character.

In combination with using various shots, you should use:

Static Movement – The camera is stationary and does not move while filming.

Panning – The camera moves in a horizontal motion. From left to right or right to left.

Tilting – The camera is tilted in a vertical direction.

Crane – Allows you to raise and lower the camera without the shaky effect which handheld shots feature.

Dolly – A wheeled dolly holds the camera and allows it to move forward or backward to follow action. A dolly is a useful tool for a chase scene.

Zoom – Zooming is a form of movement and allows you to get closer to the subject(s).

Handheld – Handheld shots are great for action sequences and allow for faster movement.

Panning shots create motion by the movement of the camera from left to right or low to high (vertical and horizontal motion). Tilting shots creation motion by the upward or downward movement of the camera on its axis. Panning adds depth to a scene while tilting the camera adds detail. In a two way way interaction it is important to place the camera in the proper location. The camera or cameras should be placed behind the shoulder of each person in a two person interaction. This way, both of the individuals are seen as well as the faces of both individuals are recorded. During editing, cutting between shots becomes easier. Do not use camera shots where an individual walks in to the camera resulting in the viewing audience becoming uncomfortable. Do not use camera shots that are shaky and affect the quality and absolutely do not film in a poorly lit environment. Do not use camera shots that have erratic movement. The more simple the camera shots are, using far, mid, and close shots with a combination of panning and tilting, the more professional your production will be. Simplicity and minimalism should be the rule in filming rather than the exception. When using a sequence of shots, they should be done in a short and brief manner. Rule of 3 is an excellent rule that you should memorize. 3 Shot sequences are clean, efficient, and professional. The Rule of 3 will help you create professional films. A 3 Shot sequence is best used as a transition between scenes. Transitions should be used between scenes to create continuity. Transitions make the film look more professional. Transitions allow for switching between scenes in a smooth manner. There are various transitions that can be used and they include:

1. Cuts – Start/Stop Recording

2. Wipes – Left to Right or Right to Left.

3. Fade (In/Out) – Blends shots together.

4. Dissolve – Used in dream sequences and flashback sequences to separate the current time from the past or future.

5. Fade Dissolve – One shot fades in while the current shot dissolves.

6. 2 Shot Sequence – 2 Fast angle shots.

7. 3 Shot Sequence – 3 Fast angle shots.

3 Act Story Arc

Every story you have heard since you were a child has used the 3 Act Story Arc. The 3 act story arc is important because it brings the audience from an introduction that presents the characters to a conflict that reveals the protagonist and antagonist to a resolution that provides a conclusion and successful resolution. Everything is about the successful resolution. This successful resolution is what moviegoers refer to as the Happy Ending. A movies finishes in a happy way because the conflict was successfully resolved by the protagonist. The protagonist defeats the antagonist bringing about a successful resolution that creates the effect of a Happy Ending in the minds of the moviegoers. The 3 Act Story Arc was made famous by English playwright William Shakespeare but it is much older than him. Storytelling is a part of the human experience and human culture. All cultures everywhere have traditions that have been orally passed on by storytelling. At one point it was recorded on parchment and written down and passed on through the literate. The 3 Act Story Arc is closely associated with Hollywood movies and it became a formula that spread overseas. Stories are more than anything else, a morality tale. The good guy wins and the bad guy loses. That is what it has always been. Can you change the formula? No. You cannot change the formula because there has to be a successful resolution for the moviegoers. Without this successful resolution, the moviegoer will feel cheated. If the protagonist doesn't defeat the antagonist then there is no successful resolution, which means no Happy Ending. If there is no Happy Ending then moviegoers will leave confused and possibly embittered by the lack of resolution to the presentation of the conflict in the movie. There has to be a successful resolution to the problem that is presented in the conflict stage. The 3 Act Story Arc is a highly successful format that should be followed by you in your filmmaking process. It has worked for Shakespeare, it has worked for Hollywood blockbuster movies, it has worked for Bollywood, and it will work for you. Use the 3 Act Story Arc and bring form to your moviemaking process.

What is a Scene?

The audience assumes that everything they are watching in the scene, the persons, the objects, are all there for a reason and are all there because they were specifically put there. A scene is a depiction of real life. Life imitates art and art imitates life. A scene is just showing life as it is. And as in real life where everything is there for a reason, art depicts real life by re-creating the conditions to do that. A grimy New York backstreet is real life which is why filming there gives film such an edge. A village of peasants in Southeast Asia is real life. Put in a few actors with makeup and props and you have a real life depiction. A scene is just a glimpse of reality. A memory is a remembrance of past reality and a scene is a re-creation and depiction of a past occurrence. A scene is just real life, re-shown to an audience. Everything has been put in to the scene for a reason and the reason is to truthfully and accurately re-create past occurrences. A story is not a depiction of past occurrences. A story is a collection of past occurrences. There is always a bad event as well as a good event, because that is the balance. The balance is disrupted when an antagonist disrupts it and the protagonist has to balance it. The morality tale element of movie making is directly linked to the 3 Act Story Arc in which there is an introduction, conflict, and the conflict's resolution (Conclusion). Characters are engaged and defined by this struggle but there struggle has to be based in reality. A movie about a person losing their home would be based in reality. A movie about a person about to lose their home but gets rich when they find oil in their backyard would be based in reality (12 million persons in America get monthly royalty checks from oil found on their land). A movie about a person about to lose their home but they discover rare priceless dinosaur fossil eggs in their backyard would blend fantasy and reality, making the movie even more enjoyable. It is the blend of reality and a dash of eccentricity that makes movies fresh and exciting to watch. The same way that a 3 Act Story Arc has an introduction, conflict, and conflict resolution (conclusion), each individual Scene should have an introduction, conflict, and conflict resolution. Using conflict in scenes is very important because a scene without conflict is not exciting to watch. Conflicts define scenes and make them entertaining to audiences. There are various forms of conflict that can be used including self-conflict. The character could have doubts about what they themselves want to achieve. The conflict can be with a person, a machine, or with nature. A conflict makes the audience interested in the scene and therefore interested in the movie. Serene scenes, one after another, would make you either fall asleep or squirm in your seat. A long panning shot of a lake is beautiful to watch for 5 seconds as a transition between a scene or to set the location before using mid and close up shots. You want to see and you are paying to see actors performing scripted or impromptu dialogue. The more genres a scene contains the better. Obviously you don't want to use 7 different genres in a scene but if you combine a few genres for one scene, then you can benefit from their combination.

For Example

Scene 1

Man: I support you

Woman: No you don't. No you don't! You have never supported me!

Man: What are you talking about? Remember when I bought you a bicycle? Hahaha…..

This is a simple example of a conflict between two characters. If the Woman agreed with the Man in this short example, it would be a No Conflict scene. Conflict arrives by contrast, verbal contrast or physical contrast. The injection of comedy in to the scene with the line "remember when I bought you a bicycle?" was to add in one more genre in to the scene and to lighten up the scene.

Scene 2

Woman: Can you bring me a glass of water?

Man: Here you go….

Woman: This cup is nearly empty

Man: I drank the water on the
way to give it to you…..

A simple exchange between a
man and a woman. The conflict
occurs when the man drinks the
water on the way to deliver it. It
could have turned in to an
argument but it comedy was
injected in to it (drinking the water
on the way to deliver it). There
doesn't have to be a fist fight or a
hard verbal exchange in order to
create conflict, but there has to
be something that creates an
issue for discussion. Drinking
another person's water is the
issue for discussion.

The creation of conflict, however
minute, creates an opportunity for
further conversation. Conflict

creates the opportunity for interaction and exchange, which is what the Director is ultimately seeking. Conflict creates the opportunity for two way or three way or more interaction that gives value to a scene. If a scene exists where everyone agrees on everything, the scene becomes pointless and a monologue would be better. A conflicting scene provides contrast between the desires of the various characters and this provides the opportunity to create entertainment. It is entertaining to see an argument in a scene because it provides emotion and differentiation in the characters.

If you are able to have a few genres in each scene, for example Comedy and Drama, that will enhance your scenes and make them more professional. Each scene should also follow the 3 Act Story Arc in that each scene has its own 3 act arc. Each scene should give you an introduction, conflict, and conflict resolution. Moving in actors in to a real town in West Virginia is more realistic and less expensive than re-creating West Virginia in California. Even if everything looks the same, it will not feel the same. It is better to fly the actors to West Virginia and film using locals blended in with actors and actresses to achieve authenticity. Even if it is not 100 percent authentic, it has to look and feel 100 percent authentic. If you are making a movie about an oil miner turned tycoon, you would have to spend time in oilfields and use locals to bring the authentic feel. Authenticity works when you use what already exists. Harry Potter filmed in English castles that already existed. They didn't try to re-create a phony castle façade. Attention to realistic details creates authenticity and that translates in to believability. The audience wanting to connect with the protagonist symbolizes the audience accepting the protagonist. They connect with the protagonist because they accept the protagonist as being able to represent those qualities which the audience possesses. The audience is winning through the protagonist (and sometimes the antagonist) because they see the protagonist as sharing those qualities or flaws that make them human.

Planning the Scenes

You can hire a line producer or you can act as your own line producer. A line producer is the business manager for a scene, accounting for everything that takes place in a scene while providing the funding for that scene. Your scenes will be based on your story and your story is explained through your script. The script was created from your story (original I hope). Storytelling is an ancient form that has passed on traditions and cultural lessons through oral transmission. Just as there are varying acting levels, there are varying levels of storytelling. You can write your stories in a linear or modular format. When creating scenes from a story, you can create the scenes in a linear or modular format. In a linear format, you would film each scene in order as it comes up in the story. In a modular format, you film each scene in any order, and then put them in order during the editing phase.

Linear Storytelling
1->2->3->4->5->6->7->8->9->10

Modular Storytelling

7->3->6->2->4->9->1->5->8->10

It is important to take the 3 Act Story Arc in to consideration when creating the scenes. If you were to film in a linear format, then your scenes would be filmed in a manner that would follow the 3 Act Story Arc format. If you film in a modular format, in that scenes are filmed in any order, then the 3 Act Story Arc would reveal itself after the film has been edited in the proper order. The first scene should be an eye-catching scene that foreshadows the theme of the movie while creating interest so that the viewing audience will want to watch the rest of the film. James Bond films are famous for creating exciting and extravagant action filled opening film scenes that stimulate mass interest. The point of everything you are doing is to generate enough interest to generate sales. That is why you are making a movie, correct? The first scene, may turn out to be among the most expensive and most well planned scenes in your film, and that is because it is the scene that will generate interest in the viewing audience, causing them to want to watch the rest of the movie. The more time you put in to your first opening scene, the greater the attention you will receive. The opening scene has to engage the audience in the rest of the movie. Whether you follow the linear form of storytelling or modular form, make sure that your first scene sets the tone for the rest of your film. Be exciting and get the audience excited! If you create a boring tempo then the audience will be lulled to sleep with that boring tempo you presented them. Everything comes down to the opening scene (some will argue the opposite and say everything comes down to the final scene but I disagree). The opening scene will set the tempo, pace, and theme of your movie, which is why it should be your most important scene.

Locations

Picking locations that could save you time and money is important. When working with a limited budget, you are limited to free locations. You have to take advantage of public areas (know where you can and cannot film legally) such as parks, universities, colleges, public squares, public festivals, and other publicly owned areas. Private areas require permission from the property owner. If you are able to find one or two property owners that will allow you to film for free, that will greatly help your production. If they won't allow filming for free, you can offer deferred pay and film credits. Whether you barter, get it free, or pay money, you have to pick a location that is not only convenient and accessible, but more importantly a location that is relevant. When you are planning scenes, the scene of the location can raise or lower the price of your film production. You should have Film Insurance to prevent from being sued if any damage does occur to a location for a film shoot. Film Insurance can, depending on the size of your film production, cost anywhere from $600 a week to hundreds of thousands of dollars. A fight scene can be filmed in a public park but if your production will create traffic problems, you will need some type of film permit. The last thing you want is to have your film production shut down because you didn't have the proper permits prepared beforehand. Let us say you are planning to film a movie about a

Samurai in a forest that saves a stranded child. You would surely have to put in time to find the proper location. So you drive 2 hours outside the city and find the perfect location in the mountains. You have various scenes you want to film and each scene has a specific location. You would have to arrange for the transportation of your entire cast and crew, 2 hours to that location. You would have to provide catering for your cast and crew. You would have to setup portable trailers. You would need electricity, so you would most likely need a portable generator. You would need access to a local market to purchase anything you would need. The farther the location, the more logistically difficult and more cost intensive it is. You could decide you want to film in Paris, France, but if your budget is $500, then it is unlikely that you will be able to fly even one person from your cast and crew there. The farther the location, the more likely that you will have to provide sleeping accommodations for your cast and crew. A 2 hour drive may seem short, but after spending 16 grueling hours filming on a forest set, a 2 hour drive back home becomes nearly impossible. It is unlikely that you will be able to convince your entire cast and crew to sleep in a tent, so you would have to have access to a nearby motel or lodge, and that means rising expenses. Locations should be picked as close as to everyone, so as to prevent time and money being wasted. The closer the location of the set, the easier it is to service. A distant location creates various problems that may completely shut down a film production. It is best to scout for locations that are close and accessible. Filming in a location outside a soundstage or backlot has several advantages. The first and most important advantage is that you do not have to build a set (depending on what you are filming). Soundstages are controlled environments where a set designer creates a set that is used as the backdrop for the scenes. Soundstages are expensive to rent but they have the advantage of offering props and various services for your film. Soundstages have the advantage of allowing you to design the set that you want and in some cases they already have various sets available to choose from. Major film companies like Universal Studios and Paramount make money from providing various services to independent filmmakers such as sets, soundstages, and post-production. You can even have your movie premier at Paramount. Location selection ultimately comes down to scouting multiple locations, choosing the possible locations, and entering in to negotiations to secure the said locations for your required dates. The more you spend time scouting the more opportunities you will have available to choose from. Your problem is not having a lack of available locations. The problem is being able to discriminate between locations and picking the one most optimal to begin planning a film shoot. After you have negotiated and secured the filming dates, you can prepare your equipment, crew, cast, film permit, insurance, and other items.

Film Permit

You do not need a film permit to film on private property. You do need the permission of the private property owner so that you are not trespassing. In some States such as Louisiana, you do not need a Film Permit (except in New Orleans) to film. In California, you can get a Film Permit for a few hundred dollars a day. In Las Vegas, you can get a Film Permit for $60 for an entire week. Even if you have a Film Permit, you can only film in areas that are designated public. Some areas of the sidewalks of Las Vegas are private because they are controlled by the Hotel joined to it. Even if you have a film permit, you cannot film wherever you wish. You should ask for a highlighted map with areas that can be filmed in legally. Once you receive your film permit, if you are questioned by Police, you can present your Film Permit and go on with your film production without difficulty. In a place like Las Vegas, it is highly improbable that you will get stopped but not having a film permit could mean your equipment being seized or worse. Guerrilla Filming (filming without a permit) is tempting to do but the consequences could be fines, arrest, and the seizure of your equipment as evidence. You should spend time researching the States and areas in which a film permit is not needed. You should have a thorough understanding of the laws of film permitting in your location so as to known the advantages or disadvantages to filming locally. The farther you film from your home or headquarters, the more expensive it will be for you. If you live in Los Angeles as I have for 30 years, then driving 5 hours to Las Vegas is not too problematic. It is easy to film in Vegas because acquiring a film permit is inexpensive and is issued quickly. I would recommend Las Vegas for filming because of its flashy backdrop and exciting atmosphere. I would also recommend Las Vegas as a suitable location because of the ease in acquiring a film permit. With a few phone calls and a few emails, you can get a film permit in Las Vegas for a small shoot for under $100. Los Angeles film permits are much more expensive and have laws such as no filming within a 5 mile radius of a major film studio (Studio Zone). Los Angeles film permits require daily official observers that just charge $200 per day. For an independent filmmaker, $200 a day is money that could be spent paying for cast, crew, and catering. This is why many film production companies, despite being based in Los Angeles, travel outside of Los Angeles and California to film. It doesn't make sense for an independent filmmaker to pay anything extra when they do not have to. Las Vegas is a few hours away by car and Louisiana is a few hours away by plane. Independent film producers will continue to seek out areas that have no film permits and that have the least amount of bureaucracy. Red tape create delays and delays create burgeoning costs. Online film permitting is becoming normalized and the amount of time to get film permits have been significantly reduced as a result of these e-government measures. Filming in a location has to make financial sense for a film production company and areas that charge more risk pricing themselves out of the film market. Multiple States in the United States are competing for film productions because a film production brings jobs and money to nearby communities.

Film Festivals

Film Festivals act as the testing ground for up and coming filmmakers, allowing them to showcase their talent to larger audiences. Few have gotten rich from starting a film festival but many have gotten rich by getting famous from their film being shown in a film festival. Film Festivals are a fantastic opportunity for you to showcase your work. You should take advantage of this golden opportunity to meet people in the industry, hand out and receive business cards, and to market your films. Entry fees to Film Festivals are usually not expensive as they are viewed by various communities as landmarks. Winning an award at a film festival dramatically raises the movie's chances of being licensed or purchased by companies such as Netflix or Amazon Studios. Film festivals, such as the Sundance Film

Festival, are active scouting grounds for film companies. Film Festivals allow you to gauge the reaction of various audiences before you start the distribution of your movie. It is a way to test your movie without any danger of negative press affecting your showing. Other than being a form of a cinematic trade show, the film festival acts as a conduit for you to find new business opportunities. Film Festivals should be researched and entered in to, with the hopes of winning recognition or an award, that can help boost the future sales of your movie. Some filmmakers like Roberto Rodriguez and Quentin Tarantino became wildly famous through film festivals, allowing them to reach enough notoriety to be offered movie production deals. The film festival is the least expensive way for a new filmmaker to build a name. It allows you to grow your name and achieve fame, if your movie is able to stand out from the rest. If you are able to achieve fame through the showing of an independent film, that will carry over in your career and act as a force multiplier in your filmmaking endeavors. Film Festival awards are important which is why companies make a big deal out of listing those awards on the cover of their independent film. It will help them achieve fame, it will help them achieve sales, and it will help create word of mouth marketing for their film. Winning an award is an important achievement for a filmmaker and it should be listed on the film in question.

Distribution

There are many different channels or avenues for the distribution of your film. You should immediately create a listing on IMDB (Internet Movie Database) as soon as soon you are in pre-production. Using a simple search on Google or Bing or on any Search Engine, you can find many independent and major film distribution companies. Satellite Television channels do pay a licensing fee to show your movie. You are usually paid each time the movie is shown. You have to email them or message them on LinkedIn in order to receive a reply. If you upload a short sample (video clip) of your movie on YouTube, you will be able to present that link in your email or message to distributors. You have to be pro-active and contact multiple distribution companies (maybe 100 or more) in order to receive back a few interested responses. Film aggregators can help distribute your film to many different venues for a fee of a couple thousand dollars. You save time and money by using film aggregators as they automate the distribution process so that you could focus on marketing. You could attempt to distribute to each individual film channel but that takes more time. The advantage in putting in the time to do this is that you are able to distribute your film to a much larger audience. Ultimately, your goal should be having as many people as possible watch your film. Using aggregators, you can take a shortcut and save time and money. If you also put in the time to individually distribute to TV networks, you will be able to reach a larger audience. Depending on the distribution company you will use the commission percentage varies. Some distributors will seek a 50/50 split, some distributors will seek money upfront, and some distributors will provide larger commissions. It is up to you to sift through various distributors and to make a distribution list so that you understand where your film currently is being shown. There is no use in going through the time and cost intensive process of making a film if no one is to watch it. Many producers will not make a movie they have not secured distribution for it beforehand. If you are able to sell the distribution rights to various nations in the development and pre-production stages, you will be able to raise a considerable amount of money for your production while confident that the distribution channels have been prepared beforehand. Everything comes down to the distribution and some film investors would like to see beforehand that the distribution has been secured before the filmmaking process begins. Distribution will be the defining factor that determines the success or failure of your movie. A great movie, no matter how great it is, will be limited by its distribution channels. The wider your distribution channels, the wider your audience. What is the point of your movie? For as many people to see it as possible. There is no point in making the greatest movie in the world only to have it hidden in a drawer. You have to make it available to the most amount of people at the same time. Distribution is about making what you advertise available to watch. Distribution is what leads to sales. No distribution, no sales. Weak distribution, weak sales. Wide distribution, wide sales (with the correct marketing campaign to make people aware of your film). Film sales comes down to distribution and marketing. If you have the distribution setup so that your movie can be found, it is up to you to make people aware that your movie exists. You have to spend all of your time in marketing after the distribution is setup. If they are unaware of its existence because you were hesitant in spending money for advertising and marketing, then your movie will not be seen and sales will not result. You have to make people aware of your movie. Distribution comes before the final stage which is marketing. Distribution is just stocking the shelves. It is up to your marketing to be able to make people know about your movie so that they will want to see it. Marketing involves time and money and can be expensive based on the method of marketing that you use. Certain marketing channels like Social Media are obviously free but others require capital expenditure.

Marketing Your Movie

Market! Market! Market! You should spend most of your time in marketing, after the film is ready for distribution. Even from the development and pre-production stages, you should also be marketing. Always be marketing. Marketing is the difference between and unknown film and a known one. The name of your movie is equally important to your success as the steps you take to market it. Everything is in a name. A movie with a sub-standard name may be difficult to market. The easier the name is to remember the more it will be remembered by people that see your advertisements. You should have a name that represents and sums up your movie. When naming a movie you want to avoid making these mistakes:

1. Use a name that is already being used by another movie. Search IMDB and verify that your movie name is unique and is not being used.

2. Do not create a name that is generic. A generic movie name doesn't stick in the mind of the moviegoer. Try to create a unique name, the more unique the better.

3. Try to avoid using shocking language in the name of the movie.

4. Pick a movie name that will create attention and interest.

5. Don't pick names that insult or offend others.

Before you set about marketing your movie, you should determine who the target audience is. What are the demographics of this target audience? Let us say that it is a movie geared towards college students. You would attempt to market specifically to them using various marketing channels including but not limited to:

1. YouTube

2. Instagram

3. Tik Tok

4. Tumblr

5. WordPress

6. Blogger

7. LinkedIn

8. Facebook

9. Flickr

10. Pintrest

11. DeviantArt

12. Periscope

13. SnapChat

14. Spreaker

15. SoundCloud

16. Eventbrite

17. Craigslist

You would use:

1. Images

2. Videos

3. Press Releases

4. Interesting Questions

5. Giveaways

6. Merchandise Offers

7. Memes

Your goal is to create interaction between your brand and the fans of your products. You want people to comment and interact. You want to get people involved. In order to do that you use interesting question, giveaways, and merchandise offers. Images, videos, and press releases are more one way communication despite them being able to generate interaction. You should have a Social Media Marketing Manager posting images, videos, press releases, questions, giveaways, merchandise offers, and memes. You should create constant content and constant communication in order to build a following. You keep your following by posting meaningful content. You keep and grow your followers by engaging with them through replying to their comments. The more you engage with your followers, the more loyalty you will build with your brand. It is important to be courteous, polite, respectful, and helpful. Treat everyone with respect but ask troublemakers and disruptors to be escorted out. It is important to not become angry and quarrel with commenters. You want to build a professional rapport with your followers and you have to stay calm and collected in the face of disrespectful individuals. By answering questions and engaging with them you are able to promote a friendly customer experience that will generate long term benefits for your movie.

Movie Premier

The first showing of your movie should be your movie premier. It should be a special one-time event that is planned beforehand. You should invite 300 to 500 industry insiders and influencers. You should hire a Public Relations Event Specialist that has the contacts ready to communicate with. They should be in charge of planning the event as well as making sure the guests are contacted and invited. Your guest list should include angel investors, venture capitalists, and businesspersons as well. You should also invite local politicians as well. They will have to be paid but it is a short term gig that should not cost you excessively. The movie premier is important because you invite industry insiders, influencers, and most importantly reporters of industry newspapers. It is important to create a Guest List. Call and email each person on

the Guest List and invite them
(assign to your PR Event
Specialist). You will need to rent
out a 300 person Movie Theater
for one showing of your movie
and that will cost you $300 to
$500. You should arrange for a
table to be setup with light
appetizers and non-alcoholic
drinks. You should have a printed
Program that gives information
on the movie and a background
on its cast. You should hire a still
Photographer to take pictures
and film of the event and you
should have a Personal Assistant
that can help with greeting
guests. You should have
business cards ready and you
should introduce yourself to every
guest and hand them a business
card. You should have a printed
vinyl backdrop for taking pictures
with guests. The movie premier, if
done right, should not cost you
more than a few thousand
dollars. Your Guest List is your

most important focus because your guests will act as influencers for your film and help make it known. You should arrange with a restaurant or venue beforehand for a post-premier closing event. Obviously the more guests you will have will raise the cost of your movie premier. You will have to pre-pay or leave a deposit for 50 to 100 people and it will cost you another couple thousand dollars, but it will raise your prestige and create opportunities for networking and business communication. One of your guests may be a politician that can offer your tax credits if you film in their jurisdiction. One of your guests may be a film investor that may be interested in your movie. The movie premier allows you to connect with higher level contacts and to build momentum for your movie. The movie premier allows you to generate film reviews, with the hopes that they will be positive, using the reviews as a testimonial. So many people will post on Instagram and other social media networks while at your movie premier and that will help you grow. The movie premier gives you the opportunity to use your guests as marketing channels and influencers for your film. Many filmmakers would wager their career success on one specific film premier where they achieved fame and success. A movie premier is vital to your film's success if not to your own. You should understand the costs involved with organizing and executing a successful movie premier. The movie premier can help your career. See it as an investment in your movie as well as an investment in your future.

Public Relations Specialists

You should expect to pay $50 an hour for a professional Public Relations Specialist with a minimum of 20 hours pre-paid beforehand. To make your movie launch successful, you have to hire a professional public relations specialist. They have access to hundreds if not thousands of media channels and they can help create a "buzz" for your film. All actors, actresses, directors, and Hollywood celebrities use Public Relations Specialists and this means that there is a large pool of individuals that already have the contacts and experience to help you. Use your Public Relations Specialist to create word of mouth marketing as well as to contact influencers in the industry to introduce to them your movie. Sometimes, you only get one chance to make a good impression and making the best impression is best left to an individual that understands how perceptions are shaped. Public Relations is not about writing a press release and sending it out. Public Relations is about relationships that have been developed over time with media outlets and reporters. A phone call to a reporter goes much farther than sending out boiler plate template press releases to a hundred reporters. Send one press release to a reporter at the Hollywood Reporter and then call and speak with that reporter. You have to attempt to build long term relationships with reporters and you should manage those relationships through constant communication. Reporters are people like anyone else and if you are establish a professional working business relationship with them it will greatly assist you in your career. Since public relations is not a one time affair, you have to put in time to developing the relationships with reporters over time. Your success will depend to a large extent on your ability to do this. Public Relations is done individually not en masse. The message of the public relations is just as important as how you deliver it. The message has to be shaped so that it has the legitimacy and soberness of a newspaper article. The message has to be created in order to shape the perception of readers. You have to know what perception you are trying to create. Unless you have full understanding of the perception you want to create you should not deliver the message. The perception you are attempting to create has to help your movie sell and it has to help you differentiate yourself in the movie industry. Everything you are doing is in order to shape the perception of the moviegoer.

With the correct perception shaping message you can create a place for your movie in the industry. Public Relations is not a one time affair. Public Relations has to be a Program and within that Program there are Campaigns. Each Campaign has the goal of achieving a certain thing such as building on the momentum of its last published press release. It will cost you $50 an hour for the services of a professional Public Relations Specialist but it is well worth it. A good public relations campaign can be the difference between your success and your stagnation. You need to get radio interviews. You need to get television interviews. You need to speak with reporters. A public relations specialist can arrange all of these for you and save you the time and effort of doing it yourself (you would not know where to begin). By using a professional public relations specialist, you will have many doors opened for you that you could not possibly open on your own. They have the contacts and the capability to make the connections and to advance your career.

IMDB

The Internet Movie Database is a great resource for you to find contacts in the movie industry. If you do not have an IMDB profile you should have one created for you or create one yourself. Any movie you are working on, whether in development stage or pre-production stage, should be listed on IMDB. IMDB allows you to find the contact information of Talent Agents and Management companies. IMDB allows you to know which movies are in pre-production and which actors or actresses are playing in up and coming movies. You can discover which actors and actresses have rising or falling careers. You can see which actor rose and fell in the last week alone. It is an invaluable source of information for the film industry. You can find information on just about any movie ever created. It is a fantastic resource for filmmakers and it is a great tool that allows you to list your films regardless of the stage they are in. Sign up for IMDB and make your profile and list your film credits. Many actors and actresses have been discovered by a talent agent using IMDB. It is used by industry professionals which is why you should start using it today. If used correctly, IMDB can be a great networking tool for meeting individuals in the industry. Use it to showcase your talent, your films, and your production company.

Talent Agents

Talent Agencies are companies that make a commission from referring to actors, directors, and talent to casting directors. Many filmmakers act as their own talent agent and find access to "breakdown sheets". Breakdown sheets are public requests made a casting director that is specifically seeking talent. Because talent agencies pay for this information, you will benefit by having a talent agent. You can find breakdowns yourself but they will be limited. Each breakdown sheet puts out a request that is answered by various talent agents or talent agencies representing talent. Each talent agent stuffs an envelope with a copy of the breakdown sheet and the headshots and resumes of the talent that matches the talent requested in the breakdown sheet. The envelope is sent to a casting director. If the casting director is interested, the casting director will give you an audition time. After the initial audition, if you are called again by the casting director it is known as a "Callback". In a callback situation, there is a good likelihood that you will get the position because the number of persons you are competing with has been reduced. If you are able to do what a talent agent does, then you do not need a talent agent. But if you are unable to access breakdowns, unable to contact casting directors, and unable to find auditions, then it is better for you if you have a professional talent agent represent you. Even if you do not actively use a talent agent, it is more professional to a film production company if you have representation. In many cases a film production company will only legally deal with your talent agent. It certainly won't hurt you to have talent agent representation as a good talent agent can open doors in your filmmaking career. Some talent agents have the ability to make or break an actor's career. You should find a talent agent that understands what you are looking for and works with you to represent your interests in that goal. Not all talent agents are alike. Some have no time and some have too much time on their hands. It is best if you meet the talent agent in person and get to know where they stand in regards to really working hard to represent you. The more you work, even small parts, get you access to better talent agents. Finding the right talent agent that is able to give you the attention and care you are after is a search that takes patience and time. It may take a few years to find that talent agent but it is worth the meticulous search.

What you should have:

1. Headshot photograph taken by a professional photographer.

2. Resume with your past experience as well as your education. Cab be printed on the back of your Headshot or it can be stapled to the back of your Headshot.

3. Cover Sheet with a short introduction to get the attention of the Talent Agent or Casting Director you're contacting.

4. Positive Attitude is essential to progressing in your career. Believe in yourself and maintain an upbeat positive attitude.

5. Self-confidence and belief
    that you will be successful,
    whether you are chosen or
    not chosen.

6. Fun mindset – You should
    be lighthearted and take
    everything with a grain of
    salt. This way, setbacks
    wont depress you and
    success won't make you
    arrogant.

7. Rapport – Build a
    relationship with the talent
    agent so that you could be
    more comfortable working
    with each other.

8. Appealing Look – Your
    acting is as important to
    the talent agent as your
    face is. Create a unique
    look that will become
    synonymous with your
    name.

Final Word

Filmmaking knowledge is gained in books and in hands on practice. No filmmaker was born with a camera. They made movies again and again until they improved to the point that they became famous for their craft. If you want to become a success then you have to have total dedication to the filmmaking craft. You have to read everything you can about it, listen to everything being said about it, and watch anyone talking about it. Most of all remember to have fun. The independent filmmaking fundamentals that are taught in this non-fiction book are nearly universal and represent my knowledge of filmmaking. I hope that you enjoyed reading this book as much as I enjoyed writing it. Get out there and start making some movies! Good Luck!

MIKAZUKI PUBLISHING HOUSE™

(U.S.P.T.O. Serial Number 85705702)

1. 25 Principles of Martial Arts
2. 25 Principles of Strategy
3. American Antifa
4. American Bookstore Directory
5. Arctic Black Gold
6. Art of War
7. Back to Gold
8. Basketball Team Play Design Book
9. Bernie Sanders Revolution
10. Boxing Coloring Book
11. California's Next Century 2.0
12. Camping Survival Handbook
13. Captain Bligh's Voyage
14. Coming to America Handbook
15. Customer Sales Organizer
16. DIY Comic Book
17. DIY Comic Book Part II
18. Economic Collapse Survival Manual
19. Farrakhan Speaks
20. Fashion Design Shoes Coloring Book
21. Fidel Castro Speaks
22. Find The Ideal Husband
23. Football Play Design Book
24. Freakshow Los Angeles
25. Game Creation Manual

26. George Washington's Farewell Address
27. GhostHuntTV Ghost Hunting Notebook
28. Hagakure
29. History of Aliens
30. Hollywood Talent Agency Directory
31. I Dream in Haiku
32. Independent Filmmakers Handbook
33. Internet Connected World
34. Irish Republican Army Manual of Guerrilla Warfare
35. Japan History Coloring Book
36. John Locke's 2nd Treatise on Civil Government
37. Karate 360
38. Karate Fighter Coloring Book
39. Learning Magic
40. Living the Pirate Code
41. Magic as Science and Religion
42. Magicians Coloring Book
43. Make Racists Afraid Again
44. Master Password Organizer Handbook
45. Mikazuki Jujitsu Manual
46. Mikazuki Political Science Manual
47. MMA Coloring Book
48. MMA Dictionary
49. Mythology Coloring Book
50. Mythology Dictionary

51. Native Americana
52. Ninja Style
53. Ouija Board Enigma
54. Political Advertising Manual
55. Quotes Gone Wild
56. Rappers Rhyme Book
57. Saba Squirrel and the Golden Acorn
58. Saving America
59. Secrets of Making Money
60. Self-Examination Diary
61. Shinzen Karate
62. Shogun X the Last Immortal
63. Small Arms & Deep Pockets
64. Stories of a Street Performer
65. Storyboard Book
66. Swords & Sails
67. Tao Te Ching
68. The Adventures of Sherlock Holmes
69. The Art of Western Boxing
70. The Book of Five Rings
71. The Bribe Vibe
72. The Card Party
73. The History of Acid Tripping
74. The Man That Made the English Language
75. Tokiwa
76. Triggering Everyone
77. T-Shirt Design Book
78. U.S. Army Anti-Guerrilla Warfare Manual
79. United Nations Charter
80. U.S. Military Boxing Manual

81. Van Carlton Detective Agency; Burgundy Diamond
82. William Shakespeare's Sonnets
83. Words of King Darius
84. World War Water

Kambiz Mostofizadeh Books

1. 25 Principles of Martial Arts
2. 25 Principles of Strategy
3. American Antifa
4. American Bookstore Directory
5. Arctic Black Gold
6. Back to Gold
7. Camping Survival Handbook
8. Economic Collapse Survival Manual
9. Find The Ideal Husband
10. Game Creation Manual
11. History of Aliens
12. Hollywood Talent Agency Directory
13. Independent Filmmakers Handbook
14. Internet Connected World
15. Karate 360
16. Learning Magic
17. Magic as Science and Religion
18. Make Racists Afraid Again
19. Mikazuki Jujitsu Manual
20. Mikazuki Political Science Manual